TOWN
GARDENS

·GARDENING·BY·DESIGN·

TOWN GARDENS

·GILL·PAGE·

Salem House Publishers
Manchester, New Hampshire

©Ward Lock Limited 1986

First published in the United States by Salem House Publishers, 1986
250 Commercial Street, Manchester, N.H. 03101

Library of Congress Catalog Card Number: 85-62899

ISBN: 0-88162-171-4

CONTENTS

PREFACE

Limited space is no great disadvantage in gardening and a small garden offers as much scope for the imagination as a few acres. Gardens are getting smaller now because of the increased need for housing and, also, because of a busy lifestyle many people actually prefer a pocket-sized garden that needs little maintenance.

It is so easy to dismiss a town garden, thinking that it doesn't get much light so nothing will grow there. But this is far from the truth and I hope this book will show you what can be achieved with skilful planting and a little imagination.

Even if you don't have a confined space you could create one within a larger garden. Surround it by walls, a fence or hedge and you will have your own private retreat when things are getting you down!

How exactly do you define the size of a town garden or backyard? Well, I suppose traditionally it can be as small as 3.7 m (12 ft) by 1.8 m (6 ft), probably walled on all sides and possibly with brick paving. But any small garden could fit into this category, even if it is only a passage way, and the same rules apply when planning and planting.

Planning to suit your requirements and choosing the right sort of plants—that is the key to success. Even if you are not the world's greatest artist it is worth sitting down one evening and deciding what you actually want from your garden—what you want to hide and what you want to see from your windows, whether it is a garden to potter in or to sit and look at and what special features would add interest. Also jot down a list of your favourite plants and if you want a predominance of foliage or flowering plants, if you want to be bothered with annuals or if you would prefer low maintenance evergreen shrubs.

There are plants to fit every situation, but bear in mind that your favourites might not be suited to your garden. There is no point in buying an expensive azalea only to find that your soil is limey and that azaleas (which need acid conditions) won't do well there. Of course this problem can be overcome by growing plants in pots containing the right sort of soil, but you can't get over the problem of trying to grow plants that need sunlight in a shady position; they will just end up pale and leggy. There is a wide range of plants, though, that *are* suitable for growing in the shade, ranging from evergreens and climbers to annuals. However daunting the situation, whether it be cold and damp or poor dry soil, there is always something that will survive there. Chapter 2 will give you some ideas.

The only thing I miss about not having a large garden is being able to stroll around the 'grounds' on a warm summer's evening. But if enough interest is provided in a small garden there will be so many things to stop and look at that the garden will seem much bigger than it really is. And it is always possible to alter things to create different effects. I always maintain that although a garden should have some sort of initial plan the best effects are created by development; by moving plants around to make different groupings and introducing a new feature that will just add that finishing touch.

There is always room for improvement and a gardener is like an artist—never completely satisfied with his or her handiwork and always looking for perfection.

A small garden can give tremendous satisfaction to the non-gardener because it can be planned so there is virtually no maintenance required and yet it can still be a pleasant place to sit in and relax. There is not the constant nagging that you should be mowing the lawn or cutting the hedges and you can go away and leave it for weeks without the fear of coming back to a jungle.

On the other hand a green-fingered person can pack even a backyard with so many plants that there is always something to do—dead-heading, tying in climbers, repotting or rearranging. The addition of a greenhouse or conservatory would ensure that there are jobs to do in the winter as well.

Your garden is a way of expressing your personality and it will tell visitors a lot about your character, from the type of plants that you choose and the ways in which they are set out, in a formal way or haphazardly. Don't try and follow other people's designs too rigidly, they may not be right for your garden and may look out of place with your house. It is a good idea to pick and choose from ideas and adapt them to your situation.

G.P.

ACKNOWLEDGEMENTS

All the colour photographs were taken by Bob Challinor.

The publishers are grateful to the following persons and institution for kindly granting permission for photographs of their gardens to be taken:
Lys de Bray (pp 10, 11, 13, 15, 17, 20, 21, 24 & 25); Mr & Mrs W E Ninnis (pp 28, 29, 32, 33 & 37); Mr & Mrs D B Nicholson (pp 36, 37, 41, 43, 46, 47, 50 & 51); Keith Steadman (p 52); The National Trust (pp 55, 58, 59 & 61); Mr & Mrs R Raworth (p 62); and Mr & Mrs W A Batchelor (pp 63, 64, 67, 69, 71, 74 & 75).

All the line drawings were drawn by Nils Solberg.

1

AIMS OF SMALL-GARDEN DESIGN

The aims of designing a garden for a small space vary according to different needs. But the basic requirement must be to have something pleasant to look out on all year round. The garden should complement the house and the design should take into account the type of brickwork or facing, colour of paintwork and any special features such as a balcony or French windows. As well as thinking about the view from the ground floor also consider what it will look like when seen from the upper windows.

Most people want an area for sitting in and this will usually be in the sunniest part of the garden, not necessarily nearest to the house. Attractive garden furniture can be made into a feature and with only a small garden to look after you should have plenty of time to sit down and relax!

Barbecues are very popular and these can be built as a permanent feature rather than having a portable one that has to be stored somewhere. There will also be things that need to be hidden such as dustbins, garden tools and possibly a compost heap if you are very enthusiastic. Whether or not you have children or pets will influence the design and also how much time you will be spending in the garden. If there is a disabled person in the house their needs should be considered at the earliest planning stage.

Many people will want to go for low maintenance and this is easily achieved with a mixture of hard surfacing, shrubs and ground cover with the odd plant pot or ornament strategically placed. Once the plants have established themselves they will cover the soil and stop the weeds from growing. All that will need doing is a little feeding occasionally and some pruning to keep the shrubs in shape.

You don't even need many plants to achieve a pleasing effect. Just a few climbers and two or three planted pockets of soil among the paving or some containers can often suffice. Choose plants with attractive foliage and which have different shapes.

If you like gardening you will probably want a mixture of evergreens, herbaceous plants and annuals. Because of limited groundspace you need to 'think vertically' and one of the first jobs is to decide what climbers you want to grow. If the garden is overlooked it is important to get things growing quickly to supply privacy as soon as possible. It is also important to think about the aspect of the garden. Most small gardens and backyards are in the shade for the greater part of the day so any sunshine that filters through should be given a clear unimpeded run.

Text continues on p. 12

Lys de Bray's garden in Wimborne, Dorset incorporates a paved area which she has filled with a mixture of plants in terracotta pots, to give an informal effect.

A well-filled garden with dense planting can make the area seem larger than it really is. Here a path in this delightful corner of Lys de Bray's garden lures the visitor on further.

Whether you want a neat and tidy garden or a jumbled one, never be tempted to plant too much at the start. Although it will give an instant effect the plants will soon overcrowd each other and, as you only have a small space, you will not be able to move them to another part of the garden. A good idea is to plant the shrubs at a reasonable distance apart, bearing in mind the eventual spread, and fill in the gaps with annuals. The better the soil the quicker the plants will grow so if the ground is poor it will pay to buy in some good quality top soil or dig in plenty of compost, peat and fertilizer or manure before planting.

Hidden corners are always exciting and they can be created quite easily. The thing to avoid is lots of small, divided areas making it look too 'twee'. A natural effect can be achieved by curving a path round a large bush or having an archway near the bottom of the garden so that you can't quite see what is on the other side of it.

A focal point is a good idea to lead the eye to a certain part of the garden. A statue viewed through an archway or a fountain bubbling up through the undergrowth will catch the attention. Sometimes it is not easy to make things look natural and casual especially when the plants are young. But as they become established you will have more idea of the finished effect and any glaring mistakes can be remedied.

With an enclosed garden you will not have to pay as much attention to the surrounding area as you would with a more open aspect. Existing trees will probably be the main external features to influence the overall design and these should be taken into consideration when planning the garden.

A colour scheme is important so that flowers don't clash and there is not a jumble of too many different colours. The whole garden could run on the same theme, for example green and silver foliage plants with pink, blue and white flowers. Yellows and white look good together and create a cheerful effect. It is the strong colours that are the most difficult to accommodate and they should be used with care to avoid a garish colour scheme. A lot of the modern hybrids are bred for their bright colours and double flowers and they often look too brash.

PRACTICALITIES

How you go about planning your garden depends on whether it is brand new or an existing one. It is often easier to start from scratch with your own ideas rather than trying to incorporate existing features into a new scheme. A lot of the old terraced houses, which are so popular now for renovation, have walled backyards which give a good basis on which to start. Many of these types of backyard look very dingy and depressing and it is often difficult to see how they can be transformed. But it is possible for even the most unpromising site to be made into a haven of peace and tranquillity in a short time—a far cry from the old-style backyards that were bare except for a mangle and an outdoor privy. These were not seen as potential gardens, they were used merely as a place of work, and it shows how our attitudes to leisure and lifestyle have changed.

With a new house you will probably want to erect walls or fencing and clear away builder's rubble before buying in some good quality top soil.

One of the major problems with the construction of small back gardens is likely to be getting the materials into it. Often the only access is through the house, or possibly over the wall, so this is a point to consider when buying large stone statues or tall trees!

CHILDREN AND PETS

If you have children you may feel that you want a lawn, however small, for them to play on. This is fine as long as you are prepared to keep it cut and have

A shaded place in Lys de Bray's garden to sit and relax in. The canopy of trees and shrubs blocks out any external features and creates an air of seclusion.

somewhere to store a mower: a small hand mower is probably all that is needed. If you are going to have a lawn make sure that it is a good one. The area should be completely flat and can either be laid with good quality turf or sown with a fairly tough seed mixture.

If there really is not enough space for a lawn you could have a sandpit for the children so they have something soft to play on.

When choosing plants go for tough shrubs, but not prickly or poisonous ones, and avoid delicate plants that can easily be snapped off. Children will need space to play in the garden so it should not be overcrowded with plants.

Children usually have bikes or toy cars on which they want to race around the garden, so any paving slabs or bricks should be completely flat to avoid hazardous bumps. Water features should be avoided as even a few inches of water can be dangerous with children about. Wait until they have grown up and turn the sandpit into a pool. Swings and slides take up a lot of space but if there is an old tree you could make a rope swing on one of the branches, making sure that it is quite strong enough first.

An informal garden is best suited to children, then it does not matter if toys are scattered about the place and they will not feel restricted as they would do in a formal garden. Also, it is no good having winding paths if you have children—they will just take the shortest route across the garden. The best way to encourage them to respect plants is to give them a small plot of their own in which to grow things.

If you have a dog, raised beds would be sensible, so long as there is plenty of paved area for it to run around in. Cats cannot be so easily restricted but you could try planting their favourite nepeta (catmint) in one corner of the garden, to encourage them to keep off the other plants.

Fig. 1. A neat and unobtrusive way to store coal or wood, incorporating a compartment for the dustbin. For best effect, use material that fits in with the surroundings.

OUT OF SIGHT

If you have a town house you may not have room at the front of the house for storing a dustbin so this will have to be accommodated somewhere within the garden. A purpose-built brick construction (Fig. 1) with a wooden door on the front can be made to fit in, if the brick is the same as the house or garden walls.

Alternatively a fence can be erected to screen off one part of the garden and this can hide all the things you don't want to see, such as the compost heap, dustbins, coal or wood stores and maybe even a washing line if you have room. Plants can be put in to cover up the bricks or fencing.

A small shed might be necessary if you have no garage or basement for storing garden tools, garden furniture etc. With sufficient plant screening a shed will fit quite happily into the scene provided it is kept in good order with wood preservative.

You may also want to hide an unsightly view, possibly a neighbour's unkempt yard or an ugly building. Quick-growing evergreen plants will be needed, but don't fall into the trap of planting Leyland cypress; they will certainly grow fast but they will get out of

Text continues on p. 18

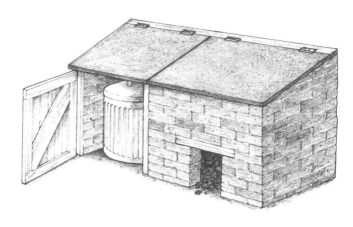

This boundary wall in Lys de Bray's garden is well hidden with shade-loving shrubs and a variegated ivy clings to the brickwork. The tree stump in the foreground adds interest.

Fig. 2. Tranquil and uncluttered—a Japanese garden maintains the correct balance between plants and hard surfacing.

A cottage-garden atmosphere is easily created and requires little maintenance. The eucalyptus in the background provides a foil for the low-growing herbaceous plants, dotted among the paving slabs (courtesy Lys de Bray).

17

hand in a small area and completely dominate the scene. There are other evergreen shrubs that can be used—*Garrya elliptica* is one of the best and it has the advantage of being suitable for growing in the shade.

OUTDOOR LIVING

The trend now is to integrate the garden and the living area so that the transition from one to the other is less noticeable. One good way of achieving this is to have a clear roof covering a patio area with French windows leading out from the house. The same floor covering, or similar colour, could be used in the house and patio, quarry tiles for example. Potted plants in both sections will amplify the garden theme. The advantage of having a covered area is that you can enjoy sitting in the garden even on wet days when the weather is warm and it is ideal for evening dinner parties.

Even though your garden may be in the middle of a town it is still possible to create a wild effect and bring a bit of the countryside to a built-up area. Wild gardens should be allowed to grow at random and you will find that all sorts of plants will appear from seed carried by birds or blown in the wind. You don't need to worry about what are weeds and what are not; just keep anything that looks attractive.

This type of garden will attract all sorts of birds, butterflies and insects and perhaps even hedgehogs. If you provide water you may get frogs too, if there is a way in to the garden.

Another type of garden that is becoming increasingly popular is the Japanese garden (Fig. 2). Tranquillity is the theme here and the effect is provided by uncluttered planting surrounded by stones and gravel and some sort of water feature. Running water has a most soothing effect in any sort of garden and is easier to keep fresh than still water. If you have a pond you will need to create the right balance with oxygenating plants to prevent the water becoming green and slimy.

Watering is going to be necessary in the garden especially if there are a lot of plants in pots and hanging baskets. Plants next to walls also dry out quickly. An outside tap is extremely useful, preferably with a reel-type hosepipe that can easily be stored. Another method, which can be fitted when the garden is under construction, is to have an underground hose system with countersunk nozzles that push up when the hose is turned on.

One word of warning—when constructing the patio or hard surfacing bear in mind that water should drain away from the house. If you have all hard surfacing and raised beds it may be necessary to have drainage holes somewhere in the garden.

2

CHOICE OF PLANTS

Just because an area is often heavily shaded does not mean that the choice of plants is very small. There is a wide range of plants that will grow quite happily in the shade, in fact there are so many it is difficult to choose just a few to fit in to a small garden. A backyard has the added advantage of being sheltered, so slightly tender plants can be grown that would not survive in a more open situation. There are no hard and fast rules about what plants will grow in a certain spot but the following categories can be used as guidelines.

CLIMBERS AND WALL SHRUBS

Climbers are the plants to start with. If you choose these first the other plants can be selected to fit in with them. Some will climb quite happily up a wall or fence without any help but others will need some support.

Shade

Ivies will provide a good cover once established and they only need support in the early stages. *Hedera*

colchica 'Dentata' is a large-leaved ivy with dark green leaves and 'Variegata' has cream markings. *Hedera canariensis* 'Gloire de Marengo' is another popular large-leaved variety; it is not so hardy as *H.c.* 'Dentata' but should grow quite happily in the shelter of a backyard. The smaller leaved ivy, *Hedera helix,* is also attractive and good varieties include 'Glacier' with silver-grey variegated leaves; 'Goldheart', green with a gold centre and 'Buttercup' with golden young foliage. Bear in mind that the colour will not be so good if the plants are grown in heavy shade. *Garrya elliptica* is a vigorous evergreen shrub that grows well against a wall and makes an ideal screening plant. It has thick, leathery leaves and long drooping grey-green catkins on male plants. The catkins on female plants are smaller and less attractive.

If you want to cover an eyesore quickly you will not do better than *Polygonum baldschuanicum*, the Russian vine. It is essential it is grown on its own rather than in a border because it will rapidly smother other plants.

Semi-shade

Hydrangea petiolaris is an excellent choice. It is self-clinging and the flat white flower heads produce a

Text continues on p. 22

Two stone urns planted with geraniums and *Begonia semperflorens* accentuate the change in level provided by the steps. Bulbs could be planted in autumn, when the geraniums and begonias are removed, to give spring colour (courtesy Lys de Bray).

This shaded arbour also includes a small pool which adds to the feeling of tranquillity. The stone bench merges in with the rest of the scenery and is an attractive permanent feature (courtesy Lys de Bray).

lovely display in early summer. For colourful foliage there is parthenocissus (Virginia creeper) and the best variety is *Parthenocissus henryana* (Chinese Virginia creeper) which is not so vigorous as the others and clings to a wall without support.

For winter colour *Jasminum nudiflorum* will brighten up dark days with its bright yellow flowers and chaenomeles (flowering quince) will provide flowers in spring followed by yellow-green fruits which can be used for making jelly. There are many different forms of *Chaenomeles speciosa* with flower colours ranging from deep crimson to white. *Chaenomeles japonica* is a smaller variety with orange-red flowers.

The pyracantha is tough and easy to grow, if you don't mind the prickles. As well as the common red-berried variety there is *Pyracantha atalantioides* 'Aurea' with bright yellow fruits that have the advantage of not being popular with the birds. Honeysuckle will grow well in partial shade and the evergreen or semi-evergreen *Lonicera japonica* is a useful cover-up plant. 'Aureoreticulata' has lovely bright green leaves with golden 'netting' and white fragrant flowers. 'Halliana' has white flowers changing to yellow.

The deciduous *Lonicera periclymenum* flowers in late summer with yellow blooms flushed purple. 'Serotina' is the late Dutch honeysuckle, flowering through to the autumn.

A lot of roses need to be grown in full sun but there are also many climbers which will stand partial shade and still produce plenty of blooms. They flower over a long period if dead-headed regularly and make good covering plants for trellis and pergolas.

'Danse du Feu' is a modern climber with double orange flowers which last well into the autumn and 'Golden Showers' is a double yellow with masses of scented blooms. 'Zéphirine Drouhin', an old favourite with its thorn-free stems and pink, semi-double flowers, provides a welcome second flush in autumn. Particularly good for a shady spot is the old-fashioned 'Mme Grégoire Staechelin' with sweetly perfumed double pink flowers—the only disadvantage is that they are not so long lasting as the other varieties. 'Mme Alfred Carrière' (pinky white) is another lovely old variety that's ideal for a north-facing wall.

Sun

The choice of climbers and wall shrubs increases if you have a sunny wall to grow them on. Both ceanothus and wisteria have attractive blue flowers and both will need to be trained as they are not self-clinging. Ceanothus produces its flowers from summer to early autumn and 'Gloire de Versailles' is one of the best varieties. If you buy a wisteria make sure it is a grafted one because plants grown from seed will often take years to flower. *Wisteria sinensis* is the most widely grown and it has large mauve-blue flowers in late spring.

Actinidia is a deciduous climber and one variety, *Actinidia chinensis,* is the Chinese gooseberry or Kiwi fruit that is so popular now. It is often thought of as a greenhouse plant but it will grow quite happily outside and will thrive on a sheltered, sunny or partly-shaded wall. To produce fruits both male and female plants are needed so buy sexed plants from a reputable grower. The other variety, *Actinidia kolomikta,* has most attractive heart-shaped leaves with pink and white tips and it has small white flowers in early summer.

Of course I can't forget the clematis. These contain such a wide range of flowers—large and small, mauve, white, yellow and pink, with various markings. There is even an evergreen form, *Clematis armandii,* with white flowers, although it is not very widely available. Of the large flowered hybrids 'Nelly Moser' (pink with crimson stripes) and 'Jackmanii Superba' (dark purple) are probably the best known. 'Lasurstern' (lavender blue), 'Ernest Markham' (red) and 'The President' (purple with paler stripes) are also a good choice.

Clematis montana is a particularly vigorous small-flowered variety and is very easy to grow. It has white flowers but *C. montana rubens* with pink flowers is also widely available. *Clematis tangutica* is a pretty yellow and the flowers are followed by attractive silky seed heads. Although clematis like the sun their roots should be in the shade, so plant low-growing shrubs or perennials around the base.

A much wider selection of roses can be grown in a sunny position and you can choose between the modern and the old-fashioned climbers and ramblers. The modern ones flower over a longer period and tend to be more disease resistant. They include the well-known 'Ena Harkness' with scented red flowers; 'Iceberg', a pure white; 'Queen Elizabeth', pink; and 'Pink Perpetue', a fairly vigorous variety with a good perfume.

I find that the old-fashioned roses have more appeal and am particularly fond of 'Albertine' a vigorous rambler with masses of double pink scented blooms. 'Albéric Barbier' is also attractive with yellow buds opening to white and 'Mermaid' is a good candidate for a south or a north wall. It's a vigorous, almost evergreen climber with large bright yellow blooms.

In a very sheltered spot *Eccremocarpus scaber* (the Chilean glory flower) will scramble up walls and trellis. It is evergreen and has tubular orange flowers from summer to early autumn.

Another tender climber is *Passiflora caerulea,* the passion flower. It will survive in a very sheltered place and is ideal for growing under a canopy or conservatory. The fascinating white and purple flowers are produced in late summer and are sometimes followed by oval, yellow fruits.

SMALL TREES

The choice of tree for a small garden must be very carefully thought out. It is going to be a dominant feature and will shade other plants. Also, if it becomes too big it will be very difficult to dispose of. If in doubt it would be better not to plant a tree at all and just stick to shrubs.

There may be an existing tree which you will probably want to leave. A good tree surgeon will remove any dangerous branches and thin it out a bit to let in more light.

Flowering cherries, crabs and crataegus all produce medium-sized trees from about 4.5 m (15 ft). Choose one with an attractive shape that will look good in winter, such as *Prunus subhirtella autumnalis* or *Malus* 'John Downie'. Steer clear of the stiff upright growth as in the 'Kanzan' cherry or, even worse, 'Amanogawa'.

The acers (maples) are excellent small trees to grow in limited space and most of them will grow on acid or alkaline soil. Some produce large trees but there are also smaller ones with a wide variety of shapes and leaf colours. *Acer griseum* is a slow growing tree reaching about 4.5 m (15 ft). The green leaves turn red in autumn and it has flaking orange-brown bark which provides winter interest.

Acer palmatum also grows about 4.5 m (15 ft) high and forms a rounded head. *Acer palmatum* 'Dissectum' has light green leaves, finely divided, and 'Atropurpureum' has bronze-coloured leaves. They all produce beautiful autumn colour.

The magnolia is a small tree that will benefit from the shelter of an enclosed garden. *Magnolia soulangiana* is one of the most reliable. It grows about 3–4.5 m (10–15 ft) high and the lovely white tulip-shaped flowers with a pink tinge open in spring before the leaves. 'Lennei' has rose-purple blooms with a white inside.

If you don't have enough room for this one you could grow *Magnolia stellata* which only reaches 2.5–3 m (8–10 ft) and is slow growing. The white flowers are star-shaped and fragrant.

Lilacs and laburnums both make small trees. If you want a laburnum choose the variety 'Vossii' which has long, drooping flowers and does not produce much

Text continues on p. 26

Brick has been used here to add height to the garden. The raised areas provide pockets of soil for planting and there are flat parts for standing pots on (courtesy Lys de Bray).

A blossom-strewn path turns a hidden corner, with the two large clay pots containing fuchsias standing guard on either side (courtesy Lys de Bray).

seed. *Rhus typhina*, the stag's horn sumach, is also popular in small gardens although the suckers can be a nuisance.

For leaf colour you could choose *Gleditsia* 'Sunburst', a small tree with golden leaves and a round head. Then there is *Eucalyptus gunnii*, which will grow into a large tree but can be cut back to the ground each spring, after the first year, to produce new growth.

If you want to try something a little more unusual why not grow *Arbutus unedo*, the strawberry tree. It grows about 4.5–6 m (15–20 ft) high and has dark green glossy leaves and small pink, bell-shaped flowers in autumn. The orange strawberry-like fruits appear at the same time, from the previous year's flowers. 'Rubra' is the best form being more compact.

Cercis siliquastrum (Judas tree) is a small spreading tree with heart-shaped leaves and pink pea-like flowers in spring followed by green seed pods. It likes a sunny sheltered spot.

Amelanchier canadensis is a lovely tree that grows well on moist soil. It does tend to produce suckers, though, and may need pruning to keep it in shape. Masses of white star-shaped flowers open in spring followed by edible black berries. The brilliant leaf colours provide an added bonus in autumn.

If you like weeping trees there is *Betula pendula* 'Youngii' which is a smaller tree than the silver birch. I find *Pyrus salicifolia* 'Pendula' (willow-leaved pear) a better shape as it looks more natural.

Figs can be grown successfully on a south-facing wall although they need quite a lot of attention in the form of training, pruning and thinning if they are to produce fruit.

SHRUBS

In a small garden it is important to have attractively shaped shrubs and to avoid planting them too close together, thus spoiling the form. You could choose all evergreen plants but you will probably want to have a balance between evergreen and deciduous and with the right choice it is possible to have something of interest to look at all year round.

Shade

If you have acid soil you can grow camellias which thrive in sheltered, shaded conditions. One of the most popular varieties is 'Donation' with pink, semi-double flowers. 'Anticipation' is hardier with large crimson flowers and it is one of the best camellias for a small garden. Another acid lover is the skimmia, an evergreen that produces white flowers in late spring followed by bright red berries that last all winter.

Holly bushes will grow in the shade and variegated ones such as 'Silver Queen' and 'Golden King' will brighten up a dark corner. For berries to be produced you will need a male and female variety and strange though it may seem 'Silver Queen' is male and 'Golden King' is female!

Cotoneasters provide a good show of red berries in autumn and there are spreading plants such as *Cotoneaster horizontalis* (useful for covering manholes), upright ones such as *Cotoneaster franchetii* that will fan against a wall and large ones like *Cotoneaster cornubia* that will grow up to 6 m (20 ft) high. Some are evergreen and others are deciduous.

Hydrangeas like a sheltered position where the buds will not be damaged by late frosts. The lace-cap hydrangeas are particularly attractive with their large, flat flower heads. 'Blue Wave' and 'Mariesii' are both good varieties and their flower colour will depend on what type of soil they are grown on; blue on acid soil and pink on alkaline.

Yellow flowered shrubs suitable for the shade are *Hypericum* 'Hidcote'—not to be confused with the ground-cover hypericum—and *Potentilla fruticosa*. There are also pink and red potentillas but I still prefer the original yellow.

If you have an acid soil you can grow rhododendrons and azaleas. There are some splendid dwarf rhododendrons, growing about 1 m (3 ft) high, and the yellow flowered 'Cowslip' does particularly well in the shade.

The Japanese azaleas do better than the deciduous ones in shade and there are some lovely subtle colours such as 'White Lady' and 'Hinomayo' (pink) as well as the stronger oranges, scarlets and bright pinks. If you do not have an acid soil they can always be grown in tubs containing ericaceous compost, which can be bought at garden centres.

Bamboos are popular and look especially good in a modern design or Japanese-type garden. It is best to grow one of the smaller varieties such as *Arundinaria murielae* or *Arundinaria viridistriata* which are not so invasive as the larger ones.

Semi-shade

For all soil types there is the evergreen elaeagnus and the variety *Elaeagnus pungens* 'Maculata' creates a splash of colour with its green and gold leaves. For more sombre tones the larger grey-leaved *Elaeagnus × ebbingei* is particularly attractive. *Euonymus fortunei* can be grown against a wall or free-standing. 'Emerald 'n Gold' is a variegated form although the colour may not be as good in heavy shade.

Fatsia japonica is often thought of as a tender plant but it is hardy in many areas and is well suited to walled gardens in sun or shade. It can be planted in the garden but also looks good when grown in a pot. It has large glossy leaves and small white flowers in early autumn.

It really is worth growing a philadelphus if you have got room. The lovely white flowers look especially good in evening light in summer and they fill the air with their orange-blossom scent. 'Manteau d'Hermine' only grows 1 m (3¼ ft) high and 'Belle Etoile' reaches 1.5 m (5 ft) and has white flowers with a purple blotch.

Also grown for its scented flowers is the daphne and *Daphne mezereon* provides welcome colour early in the year with its clusters of pink flowers followed by red berries. It is a deciduous shrub but *Daphne odora* is evergreen, again flowering early, with pinkish-purple blooms. 'Aureomarginata' has cream-edged leaves.

The pink flowered weigela is another attractive shrub and there is a variegated form called *Weigela florida variegata*.

Hamamelis (witch hazel) flowers in winter on bare stems, like the daphne. It prefers a slightly acid soil and a sheltered position to do well. *Hamamelis mollis pallida* produces the best flowers, bright yellow and fragrant.

For early summer flowers there is *Deutzia* 'Mont Rose', a deciduous shrub with rose-pink flowers and arching stems. Then later in the summer come the buddleias with their blue, purple or white flower spikes that attract butterflies—giving them the common name of butterfly bush. Hybrids of *Buddleia davidii* include 'Black Knight' (deep purple), 'Royal Red' and 'White Bouquet'.

Griselinia and pittosporum are both grown for their foliage. The griselinia is a slightly tender shrub that may need protection until it becomes established. It can grow up to 7.5 m (25 ft) high but can be kept smaller by pruning. *Pittosporum crassifolium* is one of the hardiest varieties and it has leathery green leaves with white undersides. The deep purple flowers appear in the spring followed by seed capsules.

Hardy fuchsias will make quite large shrubs in many areas and even if they are cut back by frost they will often survive. 'Riccartonii' is one of the hardiest, growing to about 1.5 m (5 ft) and it has crimson and mauve flowers. 'Lady Thumb' and 'Tom Thumb' are both good small varieties.

If you want something a bit more exotic you could grow desfontainea, an evergreen shrub which needs the shelter of a wall. It has dark green holly-like leaves and produces tubular scarlet flowers with yellow tips in early summer.

Text continues on p. 30

These cobbles have been laid flat and set in concrete, making them fairly easy to walk on (courtesy Mrs W E Ninnis).

A concrete screen block wall makes the boundary in this Parkstone, Poole garden. The owners, Mr & Mrs W E Ninnis, have used conifers to provide all-year-round greenery.

Then there is *Eriobotrya japonica* (loquat) which is growing in popularity. It is also an evergreen with leathery leaves and will bear fragrant white flowers in winter, providing it has plenty of warmth in summer. If you are lucky it will produce yellow pear-shaped fruit.

There are several good roses for semi-shaded conditions and one of these is 'Nozomi', excellent as a ground cover plant or for trailing over a low wall with small, pinky-white flowers.

Among the old-fashioned Bourbon roses there is 'Mme Isaac Pereire' with beautifully fragrant deep pink blooms and 'Kathleen Harrop', a soft pink colour. Some of the *Rosa rugosa* hybrids are well worth growing and they produce lovely large hips after the flowers. They are more suited to a wild garden than a formal one and they include 'Frau Dagmar Hartopp (Hastrup)' with pink flowers and 'Blanc Double de Coubert' a lovely semi-double white. 'Max Graf' can be used as ground cover and it has scented single pink flowers with white centres. *Rosa moyesii* is a species rose that will grow free-standing or against a wall. It has dark red, single flowers followed by glossy hips. The variety 'Geranium' is probably a better bet for small gardens as it is not so rampant.

Sun

In a sunny position you can grow the grey-leaved shrubs such as lavender, santolina and senecio. They all produce a low mound and contrast well with pinks and pale blues.

Cistus (rock roses) need plenty of sun and do best in a sheltered place. They flower between late spring and early summer and have saucer-shaped flowers in pink, white and yellows. *Cistus corbariensis* is one of the hardiest and grows 1–1.2 m (3–4 ft) high. It has white flowers with yellow centres.

Convolvulus cneorum is more tender but is well worth growing in the shelter of a walled garden. The leaves are silver and the pink buds open to white flowers. They look similar to bindweed, which belongs to the same family, but this is not a rampant variety!

Hebes are popular and as they are evergreen they make good background shrubs. There are lots of different shapes and colours to choose from and *Hebe* 'Autumn Glory' is a favourite with its purple stems and dark green leaves. The spiky blue flowers bloom from late summer to early autumn. For ground cover *Hebe pinguifolia* 'Pagei' is useful with tiny grey leaves and white flowers in spring. *Hebe armstrongii* has golden foliage rather like that of a conifer and has clusters of white flowers in spring. Again, they are not totally hardy and may be cut down by frost.

Cytisus (broom) produces a good display of flowers in early summer and will grow in poor soil, preferably slightly acid. *Cytisus* × *kewensis* has lovely creamy coloured flowers and there is also a white variety, *Cytisus praecox* 'Albus'.

The shrubby *Hibiscus syriacus* is a hardy form which will thrive in a walled garden. It has rich green leaves and showy flowers, in various shades, from summer to early autumn. 'Blue Bird' is blue with a red centre and 'Hamabo' has pale pink flowers with red centres.

I would not suggest hybrid tea roses for a small garden because they look extremely uninteresting for most of the year but in an informal garden a place can usually be found for one or two of the species roses. 'Rosa Mundi' (*R. gallica versicolour*) is a lovely old-fashioned one with striped crimson and white blooms.

Miniature roses are becoming increasingly popular and they can be grown in containers. There are some very pretty ones available including 'Eleanor' (double pink), 'Yellow Doll' and 'Cinderella' (white).

If you want something with an architectural shape you could try the phormiums—New Zealand flax. They are quite tender and will only survive in mild areas but you could grow one in a tub and move it under cover when the weather gets cold. There is a bronze form and one with yellow and green striped leaves.

Yuccas are also an interesting shape with their sword-like leaves, and they look spectacular when in flower. *Yucca filamentosa* has creamy white flowers in summer on a stem up to 2 m (6½ ft) high. *Yucca gloriosa* is a larger plant with pink tinged flowers from late summer to autumn. But both plants will need to be several years old before they flower—*Yucca filamentosa* will usually produce blooms sooner than *gloriosa*.

HERBACEOUS PLANTS

Shade or semi-shade

There are plenty of herbaceous plants that will grow happily in the shade. *Anemone japonica* provides welcome colour towards the end of summer with its pink and white flowers, and plants will spread if left alone. Aquilegias and astilbes both have attractive flowers in subtle shades and astilbes thrive in damp conditions.

Bergenia (elephants' ears) give good ground cover as well as large heads of flowers in varying shades of pink and white. Some of the new varieties such as 'Baby Doll' are less straggly than *Bergenia cordifolia*.

There are several spreading plants that do well in the shade but they need to be treated with caution in a small garden because they are so rampant. These include *Hypericum calycinum* (rose of Sharon) which has bright yellow flowers, lamium (deadnettle) and vinca (periwinkle). It is best to grow them in a bed of their own, perhaps under a tree surrounded by paving. *Lamium* 'Beacon Silver' is an attractive plant with silvery leaves tinged with pink and there are several vincas to choose from, large or small, variegated and with blue or white flowers.

Foxgloves are ideal for informal gardens and they will seed themselves all over the place. You can buy foxgloves in various shades, including yellow, but I still think the common variety is the best.

No shaded garden would be complete without hostas and they look good in groups of at least three rather than planted singly. You could mix plants with different variegations such as 'Thomas Hogg' (green with cream edges), *fortunei picta* (yellow with green edging) and *sieboldiana* (*glauca*) (bluish leaves). The only problem with hostas is that they tend to be attacked by slugs, so put some pellets down if you haven't any pets.

Ferns are also extremely popular and there are some lovely hardy ones that will thrive in a cool moist spot. *Matteuccia struthiopteris germanica* (ostrich feather fern) grows about 1–1.2 m (3–4 ft) high and produces bright green fronds with curled tops. *Adiantum pedatum* is one of the maidenhair ferns and grows 15–45 cm (6–18 in) tall and has light green drooping fronds and purple stalks. For contrast *Cyrtomium falcatum* (Japanese holly fern) has shiny pointed leaves and grows 60–90 cm (2–3 ft) tall. Many ferns will die back in winter, leaving just the crowns visible.

Another 'must' is the euphorbias. My favourite is *Euphorbia polychroma* which grows about 45 cm (18 in) high and has clusters of yellow flowers in early spring. *Euphorbia robbiae* grows slightly taller and also has yellow flowers which are in bloom from late spring to summer. There is a red flowered one, *Euphorbia griffithii* 'Fireglow'.

Geraniums—not to be confused with pelargoniums that are grown as house plants and bedding plants—are easy to grow and flower over a long period during the summer. 'Johnson's Blue' has lovely bright, single flowers and 'Wargrave Pink' has pretty single blooms. There is also a good double variety, *grandiflorum* 'Plenum', with lavender blue flowers.

Brunnera macrophylla has blue flowers rather like forget-me-nots but on taller stems and is an easy plant to grow. Another blue flowerer is *Tradescantia virginiana* 'Isis', an adaptable plant with three-petalled flowers that bloom in summer. There are also purple, carmine and white varieties.

Yellow flowers will brighten up a dark corner and

Text continues on p. 34

This rustic wood bench fits in well with the informal setting, where a more modern piece of furniture would look out of place (courtesy Mrs W E Ninnis).

Another view of Mr and Mrs Ninnis' garden shows a seating area with crazy paving. The small well-kept lawn sets off the foliage plants.

trollius, the globe flower, has large buttercup-type blooms and does well in moist soil. *Alchemilla mollis* has attractive foliage that looks particularly good after the rain when the droplets stay on the leaves. It has masses of tiny yellow flowers all through the summer.

Hemerocallis (day lilies) are extremely adaptable plants and very hardy. There are a great many hybrids with a wide range of colours, flowering in summer, and they form clumps of strap-shaped leaves. 'Pink Damask' is the best pink-flowered form and 'Morocco Red' and 'Golden Chimes' are also worth growing.

Pulmonarias are low-growing spreading plants with white spotted leaves that are at their best in a fairly moist shaded position. The drooping funnel-shaped flowers come out in spring and there are blue, pink and white varieties. Symphytum is a similar type of plant that makes good ground cover and has red, pink, blue or white flowers.

Rather more unusual is rheum, the ornamental rhubarb. The variety *Rheum palmatum rubrum* has large purple-red leaves and tall spikes of pinky-red flowers in early summer. It needs plenty of space, growing up to 2.5 m (8¼ ft) high with a spread of 1 m (3¼ ft).

Sun

Oenothera (evening primrose) has large yellow, saucer-shaped flowers that are slightly scented and open in the evening. 'Missouriensis' is a biennial and grows about 10–15 cm (4–6 in) high. *Oenothera fruticosa* 'Yellow River' is a perennial variety which produces masses of bright yellow blooms and reaches 45 cm (18 in). Both flower throughout the summer.

Another yellow flowered plant is *Achillea filipendula* which has clusters of small flowers arranged in flat heads. 'Coronation Gold' and 'Gold Plate' are good varieties and flower all the summer. They are ideal for drying for winter decoration. Also recommended is *Achillea millefolium* 'Moonshine' with silver foliage and yellow flowers.

Moving on to orange flowers there is gaillardia with its daisy-like blooms that last all summer. 'Mandarin' is a lovely cheerful variety with orange-red flowers and 'Ipswich Beauty' is another reliable form. Both grow 75–90 cm (2½–3 ft) tall. There is also an annual gaillardia which is smaller than the perennial variety.

Not all poppies are annuals. *Papaver orientale* (oriental poppy) is a perennial and there are a great many lovely coloured varieties available. They grow about 60–90 cm (2–3 ft) high and usually need staking. 'Pale Face' is a subtle pale pink and there are white, red and orange varieties, some with ruffled edges. If dead-headed they often produce a second show of flowers after the first one in the late spring.

My particular favourites are the sisyrinchiums which deserve to be more widely grown. *Sisyrinchium striatum* is a lovely plant with sword-like leaves and spikes 30–45 cm (12–18 in) high of creamy-yellow flowers which last over a long period from early to late summer. There is also a 15 cm (6 in) high variety, *Sisyrinchium brachypus,* with bright yellow, star-shaped flowers, and a small blue flowered one—*Sisyrinchium bellum.*

The large flowered heleniums are particularly cheerful in a sunny spot. 'Golden Youth' is a lovely bright yellow and 'Moerheim Beauty' has bronzy-red flowers. Some early varieties will give a second show of flowers if they are cut back after the first ones have died off.

The perennial chrysanthemums are useful late summer flowering plants—not the large exhibition types but the smaller, less showy kinds. The Shasta daisies are worth growing and 'Esther Read' is probably the best known with its double white flowers. 'Wirral Supreme' is an improved form and has double white flowers with a yellow centre, it grows about 90 cm (3 ft) high. 'Snowcap' is a smaller variety reaching 60 cm (2 ft).

Asters also flower late in the summer in various shades of blue and pink. *Aster novi-belgii* are the

Michaelmas daisies and among the recommended varieties are 'Marie Ballard' (light blue), 'Patricia Ballard' (rose pink) and 'Royal Velvet' (violet blue). They are either double or semi-double flowers. I prefer some of the single flowered varieties of *Aster amellus*. 'King George' is a lovely lavender blue and 'Pink Zenith' is also pretty. They are longer lasting plants than the Michaelmas daisies and usually trouble free.

Worth a place in any garden are the dianthus or garden pinks. They flower during the summer months and there are old-fashioned and modern varieties. 'Mrs Sinkins' is an old-fashioned white with double flowers and 'Doris' is one of the best known modern ones with very pale pink blooms. There are a great many other varieties, some plain colours, others bi-coloured or speckled and they grow about 25–30 cm (10–12 in) tall, making ideal edging plants.

For the back of the border is cynara (globe artichoke). The flower heads can be eaten if cut when they are still in bud but if left to develop they produce purple thistle-like flowers in late summer. Globe artichokes are perennial plants but are usually short-lived and sometimes succumb to frost.

Echinops (globe thistle) is also best for the background as it grows about 1–1.2 m (3–4 ft) high. The round blue flowers appear in late summer and look good when dried for winter flower arrangements.

ANNUALS

Semi-shade

Annuals will not grow well in full shade but there are some that will tolerate part shade without becoming leggy. The best ones in my opinion are the half-hardy nicotianas (tobacco plants). Even if you don't grow any other annuals these are really worthwhile and provide a lovely show of scented flowers from early to late summer. 'Sensation Mixed' and 'Evening Fragrance' grow up to 90 cm (3 ft) high and there is now a smaller variety 'Domino' reaching 30 cm (1 ft). The flower colours are a mixture of red, pink, mauve, purple and white. 'Lime Green' is a favourite of mine with its unusual yellowy-green blooms.

Impatiens (busy lizzies) do well in semi-shade and so will lobelia. The lobelia is half-hardy and busy lizzies are also usually treated as half-hardy annuals although they can be kept over winter.

Matthiola (night scented stock) is a hardy annual that can be sown outside from early spring to early summer, depending on the weather, and the small lilac flowers provide a lovely fragrance on warm summer evenings. Lunaria (honesty) is a biennial and should be planted in autumn to flower the next summer. The pinky-purple flowers are followed by silvery seed pods which look good dried but if left on the plant the self sown seedlings can be a nuisance.

Another hardy annual is *Iberis umbellata* (candytuft), a low growing plant with white, pink or red flowers, and it does well on most soils.

Sun

There are so many annuals to grow in the sun that it would be impossible to list them all here so I will just mention my favourites.

Eschscholzias (Californian poppies) are cheerful with delicate bright orange flowers in summer and ferny leaves. Some of the new varieties are multi-coloured but they don't look as good.

Rudbeckias also have orange flowers and the single flowered varieties are most attractive. 'Rustic Dwarfs Mixed' grow about 60 cm (2 ft) high and have orangey-brown flowers with brown centres. 'Irish Eyes' is golden yellow and grows 75 cm (2½ ft) high. There is a newer variety called 'Goldilocks' with double or semi-double flowers but I prefer the single-flowered varieties.

Particularly suited to a dry sunny spot are the

Text continues on p. 38

A close up view of the paved area in this garden owned by Mr & Mrs D. B. Nicholson. The combination of bricks and cobbles works very well and the terracotta pot, on a pedestal, makes an interesting focal point.

Mr & Mrs Nicholson have packed plenty of colourful plants into a sunny part of their small yet charming London garden. The bottom half, shaded by a tree, is filled with foliage plants and a trellis lends a hand to the climbers.

gazanias, low growing half-hardy annuals with brightly coloured daisy-like flowers. 'Mini-Star' is bright yellow and there are also mixed colours, all flowering in summer.

Limnanthes douglasii is called the poached egg plant because of its yellow-centred flowers with white edging. It is a hardy annual and can be sown outdoors in spring or autumn.

Mesembryanthemums are small plants with a big name. They are ideal for growing in a raised bed that gets plenty of sun or on walls. They have succulent leaves and brightly coloured daisy-like flowers.

Finally, *Lavatera* 'Silver Cup'. is another hardy annual with large rose-coloured flowers during late summer. It grows about 60–75 cm (2–2½ ft) high so will need to go near the back of the border.

The hardy annuals can be sown outdoors in spring, but better results are often obtained by raising them in seed trays in the house or greenhouse, in the way that half-hardy varieties are grown. Alternatively, trays of bedding plants are on sale at shops and garden centres in early summer, but you are not likely to get such a wide choice as when you grow your own.

BULBS

Semi-shade

There are quite a few bulbs that will flower successfully in semi-shaded conditions and earliest of all are the snowdrops, which turn our thoughts to spring. They look best when planted *en masse* under trees or shrubs and can be mixed with yellow winter aconites which flower at the same time.

Daffodils and grape hyacinths flower later in the spring and also need to be in groups, rather than dotted around singly. There are some lovely small daffodil varieties, called 'triandrus' narcissi, some only growing 15 cm (6 in) high. 'April Tears' has bright yellow,

nodding heads and 'Tresamble' is pure white and scented, growing 40 cm (16 in) tall. Among the taller daffodils there are plenty to choose from, in numerous shades, shapes and sizes. The trumpet daffodils are still the most widely grown but some of the double flowering varieties such as 'Bridal Crown', 'White Cheerfulness' and 'Yellow Cheerfulness' are also popular.

The choice is not so wide among the grape hyacinths (muscari): most are deep blue but there is a white form as well. Scillas are also blue and spring flowering, the small *Scilla sibirica* is well worth growing and so is *Scilla peruviana* (Cuban lily) which flowers in early summer. Bluebells used to belong to this family but they are now classed under the name of *Endymion*. These are suitable for wild gardens but they can become very rampant and difficult to get rid of.

Staying with blue flowers we have the low-growing chionodoxa which appear early in the year with star-shaped flowers. Less well known is 'Pink Giant', only growing 15 cm (6 in) tall despite its name, with pinky-white blooms.

Crocus will grow in semi-shade and provide winter and spring colour as well as those varieties that flower in autumn such as 'Speciosus Conqueror' with sky-blue flowers and 'zonatus albus' (white). Colchicums (meadow saffron) are similar to crocus and they flower in autumn. 'Agrippinum' is an unusual pink and white chequered variety and there's also the very different 'Waterlily' with lilac blooms.

Anemones are firm favourites and will thrive in a sheltered spot in sun or partial shade. The bright blue *Anemone blanda* is particularly appealing, more so than the mixed colours, and the larger 'de Caens' with their typical 'anemone' flowers are also attractive; and then there is *Anemone nemorosa,* the wood anemone, which is suitable for a shaded, wild garden, but, like the bluebell, can become a problem. The bright red *Anemone pavonina,* with its creamy centre, is more unusual.

These are some of the most common bulbs but if

you want to grow something unusual you could try camassia (the quamash). They produce tall blue spikes in summer and do best when grown in sun or partial shade.

Fritillarias are also a good choice with their hanging bell-shaped flowers in a variety of colours during spring. The snake's head fritillaries (*F. meleagris*) look good when naturalized in grass and they have chequered blooms in white and shades of pink-purple. The crown imperials (*F. imperialis*) are more showy and suited more to formal situations. They bear their clusters of flowers on tall stems that are topped by a crown of leaves. They are best left undisturbed.

Sun

All bulbs that grow in semi-shade will grow in the sun as well, but there are also a number of bulbs that must have a sunny situation to produce flowers.

You either like tulips or you don't, and I don't! Although I must admit that some of the low growing varieties are appealing and they have the advantage that they don't flop over. 'Franz Lehar' is one of the kaufmanniana hybrids and has bright yellow flowers with a darker centre. *Tulipa tarda* is also attractive, having star-shaped yellow flowers with white tips. It only grows about 10 cm (4 in) high.

The family of alliums include the onion but there are also some decorative varieties such as *Allium giganteum* with large round heads of lilac-coloured flowers on 1.2 m (4 ft) high stems. *Allium ostrowskianum* is much smaller with star-shaped purple pink blooms and I am particularly fond of *Allium moly,* a cheerful bright yellow. All these varieties flower in early summer.

The foxtail lilies (eremurus) are spectacular plants that like to be in a sheltered, sunny position. The flower spikes grow up to 2.1 m (7 ft) high and come in yellow, pink, orange and white, appearing from late spring to summer.

Lilies are also spectacular and in spite of their reputa-tion are easy to grow. There are some fascinating colour combinations—striped and speckled, orange, yellow, white, pink—one to fit every colour scheme.

A similar flower to the lily is the crinum which needs a sheltered site in a warm area. They flower in spring and have handsome trumpet-shaped flowers of white or pink.

For late summer colour you have the nerines which do best in mild areas when planted by a sunny, sheltered wall. *Nerine bowdenii* is the outdoor variety and has bright pink flowers on stems up to 60 cm (2 ft) tall. They prefer to be left undisturbed after planting.

WATER PLANTS

Water lilies (nymphaea) are the best known pond plants and they look very impressive in summer with their exotic flowers. The pygmy varieties are best for a small pond as they only spread about 30 cm (1 ft) across. There are red, yellow, pink and white ones available. Another water plant that floats on the surface is the water hyacinth (*Eichhornia*). They are easy to grow—just pop them on the surface of the water. But they are tender plants and should either be grown as annuals or brought under cover in winter, and kept in moist soil.

The submerged water plants are not as spectacular but the water violet (*Hottonia palustris*) and the water crowfoot (*Ranunculus aquatilis*) are worth growing. Both of these are oxygenating plants so they help to maintain a balanced environment.

If you have a moist area at the edge of your pond there are some lovely plants to choose from. The water forget-me-not (*Myosotis palustris*) has blue flowers in summer and the marsh marigold (*Caltha palustris*) is golden yellow. Spiky, upright plants include the flowering rush (*Butomus umbellatus*) and the sweet flag (*Acorus calamus*).

SUMMARY

Before you make your choice of plants it is worthwhile sending for a few catalogues and selecting a good mixture that will grow well together and provide interest all the year round. If you just go straight to the garden centre you will probably buy plants on impulse and end up with too many to fit into the space available or with clashing colours. Find out the eventual size of the plants, width as well as height, so that you buy the right number for the situation. Try to plant shrubs that will complement each other, in colour and leaf shape, and think about what the effect will be like at different times of the year.

Statues need to be used with care in a small garden but this one, in Mr & Mrs Nicholson's garden, strikes exactly the right balance and makes a fine focal point without being too dominant.

3

PLANTS IN CONTAINERS

An essential part of a backyard garden is plants in containers. They can be moved around from one spot to another and grouped together in different formations to provide a changing display. They enable you to grow plants that will not suit your soil conditions and, also, containers often look better in a small garden as they tend to look lost in larger ones.

There are so many attractive containers about now that we are almost spoilt for choice. Antique pots and containers of all types are much sought after and it is amazing what uses can be found for the most unlikely objects. Chamber pots immediately spring to mind and old chimney pots are also very popular. You can even buy mock chimney pots made especially for planting. Large old stewing pots, too big for modern ovens, can also be used.

Half-barrels are popular too and used to be plentiful when beer was stored in wooden casks. But now you are more likely to find modern ones, styled along the old lines. They either have the traditional metal rings or coated plastic ones. Wooden troughs and square or rectangular containers are also available.

With any wooden container it is important to treat it with an outdoor wood preservative, otherwise the wood will soon split and rot. Choose a preservative that does not harm plants.

There are plenty of terracotta pots about, many coming from Italy. Some are extremely fancy with decorative scrolls and handles but the plain flower pots will often look just as good. It depends on what you are going to plant in them; there is not much point in buying an expensive ornate pot if it is going to be hidden by trailing plants.

The only thing you have to watch out for with terracotta pots is the frost. If water gets into the clay then freezes, the pot will crack when the clay thaws out again. It can also have the same effect on the plant roots and plants in pots are more susceptible to frost than those planted in the ground.

In winter it is a good idea to put empty pots under cover but planted ones can be protected with sacking or even newspaper if it is only for the occasional night.

A lot of the terracotta pots on sale now are frost resistant. Most are unglazed but glazed ones are also available. As well as containers for plants there are also purely decorative ones such as ali-baba pots.

Stone is also popular for pots and troughs and has the advantage of needing little maintenance. A lot of pots available now are reconstituted stone or cast concrete but they can look very effective. There are all sorts of different designs from ornate ones on pedestals to plain round pots (Fig. 3).

Text continues on p. 44

A wrought iron balcony and spiral staircase makes a very attractive feature and they integrate the house with the garden. The patio doors (*left*) afford an alternative way into the garden (courtesy Mr & Mrs D B Nicholson).

Fig. 3. A wide selection of pots is available in all shapes and sizes. Ali baba pots, troughs, decorative urns on pedestals, a plain clay pot or wooden tub—there is a container to suit every situation.

Fig. 4. Old sinks look attractive when planted with alpines and small rockery plants, and they add interest to a small garden.

Plastic is less attractive unless it can be covered quickly with trailing plants, although some of the darker colours can look unobtrusive. The advantage with plastic is that it is easy to move because it is so light.

Fibreglass is also lightweight and some of the modern designs look quite good. You can even buy fibreglass reproductions of antique lead containers. Metal containers are attractive, especially in a formal setting, and good quality ones will last for years if they are galvanized. Self-watering pots can also be bought and these can be an advantage if you have to leave the garden unattended for several weeks, for example when you go on holiday.

Old stone sinks (Fig. 4) are popular and are often coated with cement to give a rough finish. But these too are harder to get hold of now as most of the old ones have been put into use or destroyed.

When choosing containers it is important to think what they will look like against the house, walls or fencing and paving. The colours should blend in with the surroundings and on the whole natural colours

look best. You don't necessarily have to have all the same type of containers, many will mix together quite successfully and an assortment of different shapes, sizes and colours add interest to the garden.

Hanging baskets will transform a garden in summer when they are dripping with colour, but don't have hanging baskets unless you know you will be able to water them every day. They must not be allowed to dry out and, as they only contain a small amount of soil, one watering does not last them long. The only exception is if you grow ivy leaved geraniums which will put up with drying out from time to time. Hanging baskets can be lined with moss or, if this is difficult to obtain, special porous linings can be bought.

Attractive wrought iron brackets will add the finishing touch but make sure they are strong enough to support the baskets and that they are securely fixed to the wall. You can also buy wrought iron plant pot holders to fit on to the wall.

Window boxes brighten up buildings and the same rules apply as for hanging baskets. Make sure they are firmly fixed to the wall and remember to keep them well watered. Bulbs, primulas, wallflowers and ivies are also suitable for window boxes, and will extend the growing period. 'Manger' type planters are often used instead of window boxes. They are made of metal and look attractive on old stone houses.

You may have a balcony on your house which would look good with plants trailing over the edge. If not, there are small wrought iron balconies just for putting plants in.

CHOOSING PLANTS

When choosing permanent plants for containers steer clear of those that will outgrow the pot in a short time. Architecturally interesting plants usually create the most effect such as yuccas, fatsias and bay trees.

Some of the small acers look very attractive in pots. *Acer palmatum* 'Dissectum Atropurpureum' eventually reaches a height of 2.5 m (8¼ ft) with a rounded head but it is very slow growing.

Camellias are also suitable and they will need acid soil, the same as rhododendrons and azaleas. Position the plants so that early morning sun after a frost will not damage the buds.

Conifers are good for providing greenery all year round and as long as you choose slow growing ones they will be happy in containers. *Chamaecyparis pisifera* 'Plumosa Aurea Nana' in spite of its large name is a small, slow growing bush reaching a height of 75–100 cm (2½–3 ft) and it has yellow feathery leaves. Many of the *Chamaecyparis lawsoniana* hybrids are also suitable and there are some attractively shaped junipers and thuyas.

Cordylines will add a tropical touch in summer with their sword-shaped leaves but they need to be given some protection in winter. Palms can also be grown

Fig. 5. Choose bold plants with interesting leaf shapes to contrast well with the style of container.

and the hardiest one is *Trachycarpus fortunei*, the Chusan palm. It grows into a small tree with a fibre covered stem and will be happy in sun or part shade. Phormiums (Fig. 5) are a similar shape and are hardier.

Fatsia japonica is another slightly tropical looking plant with its large, fingered leaves. There is also a cross between fatsia and an ivy, producing × *Fatshedera lizei*. This is usually grown as a house plant but is in fact just as hardy as the fatsia. It has smaller leaves and there is also a variegated form with cream edges.

Bay trees make very attractive container plants and they can be clipped to shape, either as a standard with a

Text continues on p. 48

45

Balconies are very useful for standing pots of plants on and for climbers to cling to. They break up the bareness of the brickwork and from them the garden can be viewed from a different angle (courtesy Mr & Mrs D B Nicholson).

The bottom of the staircase leads onto a paved patio, bordered by a narrow raised bed (courtesy Mr & Mrs D B Nicholson).

round head or perhaps a pyramid. They will do well except in very cold winters when the foliage may get frosted.

For a more informal look try growing hydrangeas. You could even choose the compost to suit the colour flowers you want; alkaline for pink and acid for blue flowers. They will need to be kept well watered and do best in light shade. The dried flowers can be left on the plants all winter or brought indoors for decoration.

If you have paving going right up to the house you can grow climbers in pots and position them so that they will climb up the wall. Clematis will be successful so long as their roots are given some shade and this can be done by planting in especially large pots or tubs with a layer of gravel on the surface of the compost. Everlasting sweet peas are another possibility. They grow up to 3 m (10 ft) high and flower all through the summer.

Grape vines can also be grown if they are put in a sunny spot and ivies are ideal for container growing. Climbing roses are also suitable.

Bonsai plants will provide interest in a small garden and many people find them appealing. They can be bought ready-grown or you could grow your own from seed or cuttings. Although they are often seen indoors they really prefer to be in the garden. The miniature effect is created by branch and root pruning to form a 'natural' looking dwarf tree. It is quite an art and if you are interested it is worth looking into it more fully before you spend a lot of money.

Succulents are often grown in sinks or other shallow containers and they also look good in 'strawberry' pots. They need plenty of sun, but apart from that are very undemanding. The sempervivums (houseleeks) are available with green or red rosettes and they have small star-shaped flowers on thick stems. *Sempervivum arachnoideum* is the cobweb houseleek, so called because the leaves are covered with a fine web of white hairs.

Some of the smaller sedums are also suitable for sink gardens and grey-leaved ones like *S. spathulifolium* 'Cappa Blanca' are particularly attractive. Many of them flower late in the summer and have yellow, pink or white blooms.

The saxifrages can be mixed with succulents and there is a wide range to choose from. The 'aizoon' varieties form a mat of greyish coloured rosettes which carry sprays of flowers in early summer. 'Correvoniana' is a good white-flowered variety and 'Lutea' has yellow flowers.

As well as being suitable for growing in pots, the saxifrages and succulents can be grown in the crevices of walls—they only need a small amount of soil.

Annuals are often grown in containers and geraniums look particularly good, mixing well with trailing lobelia. Annual climbers such as ipomoea (morning glory), *Tropaeolum peregrinum* (Canary creeper) and thunbergia (black-eyed Susan) are suitable for growing in pots and training up a wall or through other plants. They are all half-hardy annuals that can be grown from seed sown indoors in late winter or bought as young plants.

Begonias look showy, especially the large flowered tuberous varieties. These will grow in partial shade and will stand a little neglect. The 'Nonstop' variety is hard to beat, they flower over a long period on compact plants. The fibrous rooted *Begonia semperflorens* has small pink, white or red flowers produced in abundance.

Impatiens (busy lizzies) are ideal for growing in the shade and there are some very good compact varieties such as 'Novette mixed'. They flower over a long period if kept moist.

For hanging baskets and window boxes you have a choice of ivy-leaved or upright geraniums, trailing fuchsias, trailing lobelia, lysimachia (creeping Jenny), busy lizzies, petunias, variegated trailing ivies and nasturtiums. Choose colours that don't clash and pack plenty in to give a good show.

Coleus are often grown as house plants but they can be treated as annuals and put outside. There are a great many different colours and leaf shapes and they need a sunny position to have the strongest leaf colouring.

There is no reason why perennial plants can't be grown in containers and agapanthus are particularly suited. In fact they flower better in pots than when planted in the garden. The 'Headbourne Hybrids' are some of the hardiest and they have large heads of trumpet-shaped flowers in various shades of blue.

Japanese anemones will give an autumn show and so will *Sedum* 'Autumn Joy' with its flat heads of deep pink flowers.

Herbs

Herbs are a 'must' in my opinion. Pots of parsley, chives, marjoram, tarragon and sage can be planted up individually or together in a trough or tub. Mint is best grown on its own as it is rather invasive and the same applies to lemon balm. In winter pots of herbs can be brought indoors to provide fresh leaves all year round. Most herbs grow best in the sun although parsley and mint will tolerate shade. Special terracotta parsley pots can be bought with holes in the sides and these could be used for other herbs as well. If you put pots of herbs outside the back door you will tend to use them more often than if they are at the bottom of the garden.

As well as the aromatic leaves many herbs also have attractive flowers. You are supposed to cut the flower heads off chives to keep a good supply of leaves but the pink, rounded heads are so pretty that I always leave some on. Chives can be a bit temperamental in pots but the secret is to keep them well watered and use the leaves regularly.

Lavender is a good herb to grow because of its evergreen, silver foliage, and rosemary also makes an attractive plant. *Rosmarinus officinalis* 'Erectus' grows upright in a pyramid shape and looks neater than the spreading type.

Bulbs

Bulbs grow very well in containers and I have even seen crocus and chionodoxa growing in an old boot! The spring flowering bulbs—daffodils, crocus, muscari and anemones—will need to be planted in early autumn. The exception is tulips which should be planted later, in mid or late autumn.

The pots should be deep enough to cover the bulbs and leave room for the root growth, otherwise the bulbs will push up out of the pots.

You don't have to stick to spring flowering bulbs, there are some very pretty summer flowering ones as well. Fritillarias, lilies, galtonia (summer hyacinth) and irises are all worth growing. Lilies can look very exotic and there are many different colours available. Also exotic is the Canna or Indian shot. It is actually a tuber and half-hardy so it needs to be stored under cover in winter. The red leaves and red, orange or yellow flowers look very impressive.

Snowdrops, chionodoxa, scillas and *Cyclamen neapolitanum* provide winter colour and so will the dwarf *Iris reticulata* with its scented blue flowers.

After flowering the bulbs can either be left in the containers or dug up and replanted in a corner of the garden, where they should be left to die down naturally. Never remove or tie up the leaves when the flowers have finished—they will continue to feed the bulb so that it will be able to produce next year's blooms. You may think that this makes the plants look untidy, but it really is a necessary part of successful bulb growing.

Vegetables

Just because you have a small garden doesn't mean that you can't grow vegetables. Admittedly you need sun to get good results, although fruit will grow in the shade—it will just ripen later. Tomatoes can be grown in pots outdoors and there are varieties specially bred

Text continues on p. 53

Bricks provide the edging for the lawn, making it easier to mow the grass, and they also make a step down to the lower level of paving surrounded by dense planting (courtesy Mr & Mrs D B Nicholson).

Raised beds have several advantages – they add height to the garden, they are easy to weed and can be filled with good quality soil to suit the type of plants you want to grow (courtesy Mr & Mrs D B Nicholson).

A gazebo is a splendid feature, especially when framed by a canopy of greenery on a carpet of ground cover (courtesy Keith Steadman).

for this purpose. 'Pixie Hybrid' grows about 45 cm (18 in) high and is a fast-ripening variety. Then there is 'Sweet 100' with tomatoes the size of cherries and 'Tiny Tim' a compact plant ideal for pots and window boxes. 'Red Alert' produces early good flavoured fruit although the plants tend to look a bit rough.

Peppers and aubergines will be successful in a good summer and there are also cucumbers suitable for growing outdoors. 'Patio Pik' is a small plant specially bred for growing in pots and 'Petita' will do well under a clear roof.

Runner beans are also a possibility and they look quite decorative. They can be grown in a tub with canes or a trellis for support. Also try dwarf French beans, ordinary peas and sugar snap peas. The dwarf, compact varieties will do best such as pea 'Little Marvel'.

It is always good to have your own supply of fresh lettuce and these can be grown round the edge of tubs containing other vegetables. To make them look more decorative you could choose varieties like 'Salad Bowl' with crinkly leaves or 'Continuity' which has reddish coloured leaves. It is not really worth growing any of the root crops when you have limited space because they are fairly cheap and easy to buy.

Strawberries grow well in pots and look good in special terracotta strawberry tubs, similar to parsley pots but bigger, although many gardeners have difficulty growing them in this way and find they do better in large pots or half-barrels.

The Cape gooseberry (*Physalis edulis*) is less well known. It's a relative of the Chinese lantern, growing about 1.8 m (6 ft) high with golden coloured edible fruit covered in papery husks. It needs staking and should also be grown in a sunny, sheltered spot.

Fruit trees can also be grown in containers and there are now several dwarf varieties that are ideal for this purpose. When buying apple trees ask for the M27 rootstock on to which varieties such as 'Cox's Orange Pippin', 'Discovery' and 'Bramley' have been grafted. These form small plants suitable for growing in pots.

Other fruit—apricots, nectarines, peaches, plums and cherries—can also be grafted on to the M27 rootstock to make them suitable for container growing. And even plum trees such as 'Victoria' on a Pixy rootstock can be grown in a pot. Grape vines are also a possibility.

Choose self-fertile varieties of fruit trees otherwise you will need to grow more than one plant of a particular fruit in order to produce a crop.

Many house plants can be put outside during the summer—they will positively benefit from a spell in the open air and rain on the leaves will give them a good wash. Palms add a tropical touch (but prefer dappled shade to scorching sun) and I am very fond of the abutilon which has variegated green and yellow leaves and orange, lantern-like flowers. Ferns, ivies, citrus plants, and monsteras (Swiss cheese plants) can all be given fresh air so long as you remember to bring them indoors at the end of the summer, before there is any chance of frost. They can be plunged into the garden soil, in their pots, but they are then more likely to be attacked by pests and diseases.

PLANTING THE CONTAINERS

Most plants are bought in containers so it is fairly easy to transfer them to another one without damaging the root ball. Choose a pot that will not swamp your plant, although it must be big enough to allow new root growth. If too big a container is used there will be too much water in the compost for the roots to cope with and the plant will die.

There should be drainage holes in the bottom of the container. This is specially important with outdoor pots because, although you can control the amount of water you give the plant, you can't control the rain. Stones or rocks in the bottom of the pot will also help to prevent the compost from becoming waterlogged (Fig. 6).

Use a good quality potting compost and never garden soil which will become compacted. The peat based potting composts are light and easy to handle but the John Innes composts are also suitable and they don't dry out so quickly. Peat based ones are better if you want to move the containers around.

When growing permanent plants in containers you should scrape off the top few inches of soil each spring, taking care not to damage the roots, and replace it with fresh compost. When the plants get too big for the container they can either be repotted or planted in the garden.

Put the plants into the compost at the same depth as they were in the previous pots and firm them in well. Always remember to leave a couple of inches between the compost and the top of the container so that the water doesn't pour over the top.

Watering is essential in dry weather and, because of the limited amount of moisture the compost can hold, plants will dry out more quickly than those planted in the garden.

Feeding is also important because there will not be enough nutrients in the compost to last the plant indefinitely. You can use liquid feeds or a granular fertilizer in tablet form that is applied in spring and lasts all season. Plants will not need feeding in the winter months.

Fig. 6. Tubs should have adequate drainage otherwise the compost will become waterlogged. Ideally they should be raised off the ground, have drainage holes in the bottom and a layer of stones beneath the compost. Leave a gap between the top of the tub and the compost to allow for watering.

Fruit trees will need pots up to 30 cm (12 in) in diameter and vegetables such as runner beans should also be given plenty of room. Growing bags can be used but pots will look more decorative. They don't need to be fancy ones; plain clay pots can look very pleasing. Feeding is essential with fruit and vegetables if you are to have a good crop and a high potash feed, such as tomato fertilizer, will give the best results.

The very high wall in this garden (The Greyfriars, Worcester) provides shelter for the climbers and shrubs. The little wooden bridge, flanked by bergenias could be adapted to suit any garden, whether there is water or not (courtesy The National Trust).

4

HARD SURFACING

In a small garden paving will be very important because you probably will not have any lawn. A lawn sets off the shrubs and flower beds to their best advantage so you will have to try and create the same effect with hard surfacing. To decide what sort of material you want to use you will first have to look at the house walls and boundary walls or fence to see what will fit in with these. Whether the garden is to be formal or informal will also have to be taken into consideration.

There are many different kinds of paving available and pre-cast slabs are the most widely used. They come in various sizes, shapes and colours and are probably the easiest and one of the cheapest methods of hard surfacing.

Most of the slabs have a smooth surface but there are also textured ones—some made to look like setts, others with a 'riven' or layered look and stable tiles that resemble a bar of chocolate. A smooth surface is necessary on a patio where there is going to be garden furniture and is also best where children will be playing. Non-slip paving is also recommended.

Slabs can be laid in different patterns using different colours, but try to avoid a mottled, disjointed effect, and, if unsure, lay them in line with one another and use one colour.

Stone is much more expensive but is very effective especially next to an old property. It is best to choose a local stone because it will fit in with the surroundings and will also be cheaper. The disadvantage with stone is that it is difficult to lay because of the uneven shapes and thicknesses.

Bricks can look extremely attractive and are used quite widely. Good quality bricks are essential otherwise they will crack and become uneven; walling or facing bricks are not suitable because they are susceptible to frost damage. There are hundreds of different bricks, some hand made and very expensive. Engineering bricks are very good and Staffordshire blues are one of the hardest types if you can get hold of them. They were once used in thousands around ordinary terraced houses and in yards but good quality ones are costly. Brick pavers are also durable and as well as oblong shaped ones, hexagonal and interlocking pavers are available.

The bricks can be laid in all sorts of different patterns, using either the bedding face, presenting the largest surface area, or laid on their side (Fig. 7). They may also be used as surrounds for concrete slabs, if you don't want to cover a large area completely with bricks.

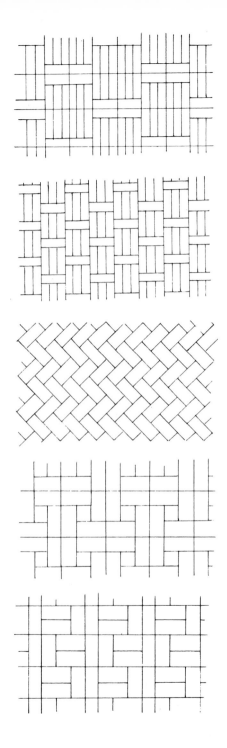

Granite setts are another possibility and these are very long-lasting. They are grey and square shaped and create quite a hard effect. If you have an inspection cover in the garden it is possible to buy a recessed cover so that paving can be set into it and it will blend in with the rest of the surfacing while still being easy to remove if necessary.

Cobbles can either be laid loose or set in concrete and are suitable for areas that will not be walked on very much (Fig. 8). They look good in Japanese-style gardens, especially the larger cobbles. Different sizes are available and they can be laid flat in patterns or laid upright for maximum 'cobbled' effect.

Gravel or shingle is very useful for filling in between paving or stones or as a surface on its own. It comes in various colours and sizes of chipping, the smallest size being easiest to walk on. It is useful as a stop gap between paving and house walls, if the paving is at or above the damp proof course.

It is best to have an edging around a gravel area—bricks or old railway sleepers—to stop the gravel getting on to the flower beds. A fresh layer will be needed from time to time as the gravel consolidates. Shaped edging stones can also be bought—semi-circular or pointed ones.

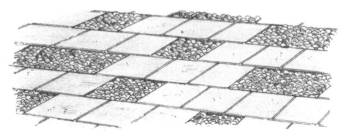

Fig. 8. Try combining different types of hard surfacing—cobbles set in cement make a paved area more interesting.

Fig. 7. (Left) Bricks can be laid in various ways to produce different patterns—laying them either face down or sideways. Here are five examples.

Text continues on p. 60

This part of The Greyfriars garden shows how a low-maintenance garden can be made with the use of hard surfacing. Bricks, cobbles and paving are very effectively combined (courtesy The National Trust).

If you haven't enough room for a proper pond you could make a small one in a wall, like this one at Greyfriars. Quarry tiles have been used in the recess (courtesy The National Trust).

For an informal look crazy paving may be laid or gaps can be left between slabs or stone to allow low-growing plants to grow through. Try and get the paving as even as possible otherwise you will be forever tripping over it.

An alternative is concrete laid *in situ*. It is often satisfactory on small areas, once it has weathered a bit, but can look stark and uninteresting on large areas. A strong mix is essential because if it is too weak, i.e. too much sand and gravel and not enough cement, it will break up in frosty weather.

Quarry tiles were often used in old backyards and front courtyards, particularly black and white ones mixed to give a chequerboard effect. There are also some attractive red colours now.

Tarmac is usually thought of as a surfacing for

Text continues on p. 65

Fig. 9. A 'stepped' effect will add height to the garden and also provide pockets of well-drained, fertile soil. You can even choose the type of soil according to what sort of plants you want to grow.

Steps with a difference – cobbles and old tiles, set in cement, are used in an imaginative way. The everlasting sweet pea in the foreground makes a colourful display (courtesy The National Trust).

A secluded corner of Mr & Mrs R Raworth's garden at Twickenham. The brick paving and strategically placed terracotta pots mean little maintenance is needed in this part of the garden – simple but effective.

This Cheltenham garden belongs to Mr & Mrs W A Batchelor and is designed along simple lines to create a low-maintenance garden with something of interest to look at all year round.

The garage at the back of the house has been effectively disguised with pillars and a water feature to give a very pleasing view from the house and patio (courtesy Mr & Mrs W A Batchelor).

driveways, but some of the coloured finishes are suitable for gardens. The easiest method is to buy dry Macadam that just needs to be raked and rolled. It is aviable in red or black, with or without chipping.

Timber decking is very popular now due to continental influences. It looks very attractive but can become slippery in wet weather, although some of the latest products claim to be non-slip.

Drainage is an important consideration because if pools of water lie on the paving they can be a nuisance in warm weather but a potential danger if they freeze in winter. If possible the water should be allowed to drain into the flower beds or if this is impractical, for example if you have raised beds, you will need a drain and soakaway.

When constructing your hard surface area you may want to incorporate a small pool. I think that formal shapes, in brick or concrete, often look better than the moulded fibreglass pools that are seen at most garden centres. If concrete is used it should be water-proofed and reinforced. Brick will need to be rendered with a waterproof facing. The pool could either be flush with the paving or raised above it.

Don't forget that an overflow will be needed, to avoid flooding the garden when it rains, and also an outlet so that the pool can be drained for cleaning.

You may want to use hard surfacing to create a change in level. Slabs and bricks can be made into formal steps and stone also looks very effective when used as random stepping stones. Railway sleepers make good stoppers for gravel treads, although it is best not to use them for the treads themselves as they will become very slippery.

Changes in level can also be made with raised beds. The edges may be constructed of brick, stone, railway sleepers, peat blocks or concrete blocks. The advantage of raised beds is that you can fill them with good quality soil and have a fertile, well-drained medium in which plants will thrive (Fig. 9). They can also be used to cover up an ugly wall or to create more height. I have seen a very good 'stepped' effect using brick walls with narrow strips of soil in which trailing plants were growing and cascading down over the walls.

Alpines, in particular, grow well in raised beds because they need good drainage. A layer of gravel over the soil surface will prevent the plants from becoming too wet and rotting.

Whatever the type of hard surfacing used it will always look better when it has weathered and when plants have grown up around it. The main problem likely to be encountered is algae forming on paving, making it slippery. There are several cleaning products specially for this purpose and they should be used regularly on areas that are walked on. On parts where you don't often walk the algae can look quite attractive on brickwork and stones.

WALLS AND FENCES

You will probably already have a boundary wall or fence, but you may want a screen somewhere in the garden, to hide something or to provide a private sitting area. Bricks or stone can be used, in keeping with an existing wall, or you may want a more open screen provided by patterned concrete blocks. Most of them look best when there are climbing plants growing up through them, although some of the terracotta shapes are more attractive. Reconstituted stone block also looks quite good.

Trellis will make a screen if covered with climbing plants or you may want to use larchlap or interwoven fencing that can be bought in panels. Choose a good quality fence because the cheaper ones are very flimsy and will not last long. Treatment with wood preservative is essential and nowadays we are spoilt for choice, there are so many makes available.

Wattle fencing is not long lasting but it will fit in well with an informal 'wild' garden.

5

FEATURES

The finishing touches to any garden are made by the strategic positioning of an ornament, a piece of garden furniture or perhaps even a greenhouse.

There are a great many statues and ornaments for sale now ranging from stone animals to large stone columns and urns. Staddle stones, rather like mushrooms, are popular; they were once used for raising hay barns off the ground. 'Japanese' stones can also be bought for a modern or Japanese-style garden. They come in various shapes and sizes and may be used on their own or in groups.

Several firms sell antique garden ornaments but it is also possible to buy some very good reproductions such as mill stones and stone sundials or lead statues. Depending on what type of garden you have, ornaments can be made into a focal point or tucked away in the greenery. It is very much a matter of taste, after all some people like garden gnomes!

New stone ornaments may look a bit stark at first but will blend in better when they have weathered. One tip, that I have yet to try, is to bury them in the compost heap for the winter. Apparently they come out coated in algae and looking as if they have been around for years!

Sculpture is popular but modern sculpture in part-icular needs to be very carefully sited to look right. It is no good having a sculpture that completely dominates the scene and detracts from the plants, even if it is a focal point. Harmony is the aim and the type of house and style and size of the garden should all be taken into consideration.

Instead of buying an ornament you could create your own features, perhaps with an interesting piece of log or driftwood, or a few boulders. Old tree stumps look attractive with plants growing up them, although you run the risk of honey fungus developing on the dead wood.

Also, if you come across any old water pumps, old gas lamps or farm implements that can be done up they will make quite a feature. And if you really want to create a talking point you could buy one of the old telephone boxes—just right for storing tools in!

Bird baths, feeding tables and nesting boxes will bring plenty of interest, especially if you spend a lot of time sitting looking out at the garden. They are readily available and some of the rustic ones look quite good.

Garden furniture is seen in most gardens and you will want to find something that is attractive and probably also sufficiently hard wearing to be left outside all year—in a small garden there may not be enough room

Text continues on p. 68

The use of pillars in a small garden could look overpowering, but these are to scale with the rest of the design and are a good way of adding height (courtesy Mr & Mrs W A Batchelor).

to store furniture under cover. Cast iron and wrought iron will last for years if it is good quality. Some of the ornate cast furniture is too fancy for my liking but there are some attractive plainer designs. Cast aluminium is lighter, and cheaper, than cast iron. Wrought iron was traditionally used for garden furniture, when blacksmiths made them as a side line. It is still available today, although a lot of seats and tables are made from fabricated steel which corrodes much more quickly than wrought iron. There are various metal coatings e.g. plastic ones which can be applied either by dipping or by spraying.

Some of the plastic coated metals are initially attractive but the plastic often peels off and there is not much you can do about that. Only buy top quality plastic coated furniture. All-wood seats are often very attractive and will last well if treated with a wood preservative. Hardwoods, such as teak, mahogany and iroko will last the longest but the cheaper softwoods, for example pine, have a shorter life. Most of the metal seats have wooden slats but there are a few all-metal ones available.

For real style there are the 'Lutyens' type wooden seats based on designs that Lutyens used in his own gardens and in those of Gertrude Jekyll.

Some of the moulded plastic furniture looks good in a modern garden and the top quality ones will stand up to the weather. Many of the patio sets come with parasols as well.

I prefer green and black furniture which blends into the scenery but white is also very popular. A disadvantage with white is that it has to be cleaned regularly to keep it looking smart.

Make sure you try the seats before you buy them—some of the most attractive furniture doesn't seem to have been designed for sitting on!

Permanent seats can be made out of brick or concrete, covering them with cushions when you want to use them. Stone benches, popular in large Victorian gardens, are often available from the same sources as stone ornaments.

Old sewing machine frames make good bases for tables, topped with wood. And blocks of stone could also be used as tables.

Barbecues have taken off in a big way over the past few years and they provide an excellent way of integrating the living area with the garden. There are a lot of free-standing barbecues available, in a wide price range, but these need to be stored somewhere in winter so it is often better to build a permanent one that will fit into the garden without looking obtrusive (Fig. 10).

Brick can be used and if you have brick paving the barbecue could be made with the same material. Keep the barbecue a reasonable distance from the house where it will not set fire to anything if it gets out of hand. A cover could be placed on top of the barbecue when it is not in use and plants could be stood on the cover to disguise it further.

Text continues on p. 70

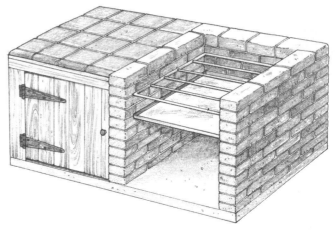

Fig. 10. A permanent barbecue, made out of brick, with storage space for bags of charcoal and utensils, and plenty of room for cooking.

A mirror at the back of the pond give an extra dimension to the scene and makes the garden seem bigger. The edges of the pond are not cluttered, but planted with a few simple foliage plants (courtesy Mr & Mrs W A Batchelor).

WATER

Most people find water fascinating and even a small pool makes an attractive feature. In a backyard there may not be enough room for anything extravagant and a small square brick pool will often suffice. Stone pools can be bought and they look better than a plastic-lined one. If you have not got room for a proper pond or don't want to have it as a permanent feature you could make a water garden in a half beer barrel. They will remain watertight if the wood is kept wet. Even if you just grow a couple of water lilies in it, the effect will be pleasing.

Still water tends to go green and slimy but this can be avoided by having the correct balance of oxygenating plants. Suitable oxygenators include elodea (Canadian pondweed), hottonia (water violet) and sagittaria (arrowhead). You will need at least 10 plants for every square metre (square yard) of water surface.

The problem will not arise with running water and a simple waterfall can be created down brick steps or over cobbles. Fountains are also very soothing and pumps to circulate the water can easily be bought from garden centres. But bear in mind that they need an electricity supply. If you haven't got room for a pool you could have a fountain coming out of a wall, a bowl-shaped one or even a lion's head.

If you want to do something a little different you could have a mural on one of the walls, perhaps a garden scene to act as an extension to the garden or something on a grander scale as a form of escapism. Or if that idea does not appeal to you don't forget that different effects are created by painting boundary walls in plain colours—green to blend in with the scenery or a brighter, bolder colour to add contrast.

To complete the scene what about some lighting—to illuminate the barbecue on a warm summer evening or simply to light up the garden so that you can look at it from inside? Light shining on to a water feature or statue will create a completely new aspect to

the garden. The lamps will need to be made of weatherproof material such as good quality wrought iron. There are many different types of wrought iron lamps, either on stands or for fitting on to a wall. You can either have a modern design or an old-fashioned one, depending on the type of garden, and there are even stone 'Chinese' lanterns available.

As well as lamps for lighting a patio area or path there are also spotlights to illuminate a certain part of the garden. They can be placed unobtrusively among shrub borders and come in several different colours.

Underwater lighting can create an attractive effect, the lamps can either be submerged or floated on the surface. They are sealed units with a waterproof housing to make them safe. Also available are 'light fountains'—the water passes over different coloured lights to produce coloured jets of spray. An added advantage of lighting is that it may deter burglars. It is possible to buy lamps with a built-in light detector so that they will switch themselves on when it gets dark.

Special care must be taken when electrical appliances are used outside and all the fittings and cable should be completely weatherproof and comply with current regulations. It is a good idea to have two-way switches so that the lights can be switched on and off from indoors.

A safer way of using electricity outdoors is to have a transformer from which 12 volt appliances can be used. Lighting systems are sold complete with a transformer and low voltage cable. This means that if there is a fault or a child tampers with the lights they are not lethal. Pool pumps and barbecues can also be run on a 12 volt supply.

If you do run outdoor appliances off a 240 volt mains supply it will be much safer if you use a residual current device, or earth leakage circuit breaker, to give it another name. These can be bought to replace a normal socket outlet. As well as lighting, an electricity supply might be needed for a pool pump or an electric barbecue.

Text continues on p. 72

The colour of the pillars and the paving is the same as the house walls, blending the garden and the house together (courtesy Mr & Mrs W A Batchelor).

If you do not want to go to the trouble of having an electricity supply run out to the garden there are now modern versions of the old oil lamps that can be bought in a variety of bright colours. They can be put on a table or secured on poles and stuck in the garden or a flower pot. Night flares are also good for an evening barbecue.

You may have room in your garden for a small greenhouse which, if it is a good design, will make a feature in itself. There are several shapes to choose from and probably the best choice if space is limited would be a hexagonal one. There are also domed greenhouses but these don't look as decorative. If you need more space for growing you might want a rectangular shape of which there are many. Red cedar construction looks the best but it needs to be well maintained. Aluminium is an alternative, it doesn't look as attractive as wood but it has the advantage of requiring little maintenance. Lean-to greenhouses and conservatories can be used for growing plants and as an extension to the living area. Some of the Victorian-style constructions look very impressive and there are small versions as well as the grand styles seen on large houses.

If you prefer just to sit and watch your garden rather than participating in greenhouse work you may like to have a summerhouse. I know they are mostly seen in big gardens but there's no reason why they aren't suitable for a small one. Apart from sitting in they can also be a useful place to store a few tools, or furniture in the winter.

On similar lines, but purely for decoration is a gazebo, often made out of fancy wrought iron work; they can even be bought from department stores now. They look delightful with climbers growing up over them and will provide a pleasant place to sit on a hot day.

Another way of adding height is to have a pergola for plants to climb up. It may be made out of timber or metal and can be used to make a covered walkway or sitting area. The construction should not be too big, otherwise the effect might be overpowering in a small space. If you want to be really grand there are pergolas with stone pillars available, but they tend to look better in large gardens.

ROOF GARDENS

Another facet of town gardening is the roof garden, which sounds very romantic but needs a lot of thought before being constructed. The main problem of course is weight, especially if you want to grow trees and large shrubs in borders. An easy alternative is just to have a few plants in pots.

Assuming that you have taken care of the structural problems you then have to decide what sort of plants you want. The garden is likely to be very windy and probably receives plenty of sun. You can choose the type of soil to suit the plants. The growing medium should be as light as possible and, if pots are used, they should also be made from lightweight material.

There aren't really any limits to the sort of plants you can grow. Of course, very big trees would be unsuitable, although it is best to choose tough subjects that can stand up to the wind. The depth of soil is a big factor and you may only be able to have shallow-rooting shrubs or herbaceous plants. If the garden is open you will need some sort of open fencing to filter the wind.

6

PLANTING AND MAINTENANCE

Whatever type of garden you choose it will need some sort of maintenance to keep it looking good. If you don't have a lawn or hedges this cuts down the work considerably, and how many plants you have will be another factor.

Plants in containers need more looking after than those planted in the garden. They need regular watering and feeding in summer and will have to be repotted when they outgrow their pots. This is usually best done in spring, using a good potting compost that is suited to the plant's requirements. Put plenty of crocks in the bottom, for drainage, and firm the soil in well so that there are no air pockets around the roots. It is a good idea to put newly planted containers in a shady spot at first (even the sun lovers) until they have settled in to their new home.

Most shrubs and trees will be bought in containers but bare rooted ones are available in autumn. Soil preparation is important for all types and it is a good idea to dig over the whole border, incorporating peat or compost. Dig a hole big enough to accommodate the roots without them being squashed up and make sure the soil level is the same height as it was when the plant was in its pot. Container-grown shrubs can be planted at any time of the year but they will need special care if planted in summer when they are more likely to dry out.

Mulches are widely used now and they retain moisture and cut down on weeding as well as looking attractive. Forest bark is a rich brown colour and goes well with all types of plants. A 5 cm (2 in) deep layer will be needed to suppress weeds. Make sure that all bare patches of earth are covered and only put the bark down on moist soil. Gravel can also be used as a top dressing in a formal setting.

Another way of cutting down on weeding is to have plenty of ground cover plants. They really are essential if you want a low-maintenance garden and they can be used to under-plant shrubs and trees. It is possible to cover all the soil so the weeds don't stand a chance!

Pruning is a necessary task and it will mostly be a case of cutting out straggly branches and dead wood. Evergreen shrubs require little pruning, unless they become too big and leggy. As a general rule deciduous shrubs that flower on shoots produced in the same year should be pruned in early spring. Growth can be cut back almost to ground level if space is limited. They will then start new growth which will carry the flowers. Those which flower on growth produced in the previous year should not be pruned until after they

Text continues on p. 76

A fountain in the pond gives the soothing sound of running water and helps to prevent the water becoming stagnant (courtesy Mr & Mrs W A Batchelor).

A good example of how a small courtyard or basement entrance can be bright and pleasant. Combinations of hard surfacing and a few plants are all that is needed (courtesy Mr & Mrs W A Batchelor).

have finished flowering, and then only old wood should be cut out.

The same rules apply to climbers. Those flowering on current season's growth don't necessarily have to be pruned down to the ground, they can just be thinned out, removing old wood. Clematis have varieties belonging to both groups so it is important to find out which variety you have before pruning, otherwise you might end up with no flowers. Most ramblers and old-fashioned roses flower on shoots produced in the previous year and so should be pruned after flowering. There are differing opinions on when shrub roses should be pruned. On the whole it is best to leave the final pruning until late winter, except in mild areas where it can be done in autumn. Any long straggly growth can be taken off in autumn to prevent wind damage.

Flowers will also need to be dead-headed regularly so that more blooms are produced. Hydrangeas can either be picked and used dried for indoor decoration or they can be left on the plants where they will look attractive during winter and also give extra protection from frost.

Getting rid of garden rubbish is a problem, especially in a built-up area where it is not possible to have a bonfire. Composting can be done on a small scale and the best way to keep it under control in a small garden is to buy a purpose-built compost container that will fit into the garden without looking obtrusive. Alternatively you could make one out of bricks or slatted wood, remembering that it is important to have a good flow of air through the compost if you are going to get good results. Prunings and other bulky rubbish should be chopped up into small pieces. If the compost is managed properly and an activator (to speed up the process) is used then it shouldn't smell unpleasant.

Wood preserving is an important part of the maintenance programme and there are many different products to choose from. The main thing is to use some sort of preservative every year to prevent wood cracking and rotting, and to use one that does not harm plants. Apart from various shades of brown and green there are all sorts of colours, including red and blue.

Pools require a lot of maintenance if they are to remain fresh and pleasant to look at. An annual clear out will be necessary, so it is a good idea to have a small pond otherwise you will have a difficult job getting rid of the old water. Algicides can be bought to clear away green slime but it is far better to have the correct balance of submerged and surface plants. If you are going to keep fish in the pond it is even more important to have clean water.

Whatever type of small garden you have I hope this book will show you how it is possible to design it to suit your needs and to gain pleasure from pottering about in it or just sitting and enjoying the surroundings. Planning a garden is as important as planning the decor for your house, to create the type of environment you want to live in.

APPENDIX: PLANT LISTS

TREES FOR A SMALL GARDEN

Acer griseum (maple)
Acer palmatum 'Dissectum' (maple)
Acer pseudoplatanus 'Brilliantissimum'
Arbutus unedo (strawberry tree)
Betula pendula 'Youngii' (weeping birch)
Carpinus betulus 'Columnaris'
Cercis siliquastrum (Judas tree)
Crataegus monogyma 'stricta' (hawthorn)
Eriobotrya japonica (loquat)
Ficus carica (fig)
Gleditsia triacanthos 'Sunburst' or 'Ruby Lace'
Laburnum×vossii
Magnolia stellata
Malus sargentii and other varieties (crab)
Prunus subhirtella autumnalis and other varieties
Pyrus salicifolia 'Pendula' (weeping pear)
Sorbus aria×hostii (whitebeam)
Syringa (lilac)

SMALL VARIETIES OF SHRUBS

* Berberis stenophylla 'Corallina Compacta'
  Berberis thunbergii 'Bagatelle'
* Chamaecyparis lawsoniana 'Minima Glauca'
* Cotoneaster microphyllus thymifolius
* Cotoneaster 'Skogholm Coral Beauty'
* Cryptomeria japonica 'Vilmoriniana'
  Cytisus beanii (broom)
  Cytisus Dukaat
* Euonymus fortunei 'Silver Pillar' or 'Emerald 'n Gold'
* Hebe 'Carl Teschner'
* Hebe pinguifolia 'Pagei'
* Juniperus sabina 'Tamariscifolia'
* Juniperus squamata 'Blue Carpet'
* Lavandula spica 'Hidcote' (lavender)
  Rhododendron impeditum
* Santolina chamaecyparissus 'Nana'

* Evergreen

CLIMBERS FOR NORTH AND EAST FACING WALLS

      Chaenomeles varieties (quince)
      Clematis varieties
*   Euonymus varieties
*   Garrya elliptica
*   Hedera varieties (ivy)
      Hydrangea petiolaris
      Jasminum nudiflorum
      Jasminum officinale
      Lonicera japonica 'Aureoreticulata' (honeysuckle)
      Parthenocissus (Virginia creeper)
      Polygonum baldschuanicum (Russian vine)
*   Pyracantha varieties

SHRUBS FOR GROWING IN CONTAINERS

*   Acer palmatum 'Dissectum Atropurpureum' (maple)
*   Arundinaria viridistriata (bamboo)
*   Camellia varieties
*   Chamaecyparis pisifera 'Plumosa Aurea Nana'
*   Cordyline
*   Elaeagnus varieties
*   Euonymus varieties
*   ×Fatshedera lizei
*   Fatsia japonica
*   Hebe varieties
      Hydrangea
*   Laurus nobilis (bay)
*   Lavandula (lavender)
*   Phormium (New Zealand flax)
*   Trachycarpus fortunei (Chusan palm)
*   Vinca (periwinkle)
*   Yucca

GROUND COVER PLANTS FOR SHADY CONDITIONS

*   Bergenia (elephants' ears)
      Epimedium
*   Euonymus fortunei
*   Hedera (ivy)
      Hosta
*   Hypericum calycinum (rose of Sharon)
*   Lamium (dead nettle)
*   Pachysandra terminalis
      Polygonum affine
      Pulmonaria (lungwort)
*   Vinca (periwinkle)

BEDDING PLANTS FOR THE SHADE

      Antirrhinum
      Begonia semperflorens
      Fuchsia
      Impatiens (busy lizzie)
      Myosotis (forget-me-not)
      Nicotiana (tobacco plant)
      Petunia
      Primula
      Tropaeolum (nasturtium)

*   Evergreen

INDEX